KT-145-128

SUPER SPORTS
MOUNTAIN SPORTS

DAVID JEFFERIS

Chrysalis Children's Books

▲ Using a rope to go down a rock face is called abseiling.

First published in Great Britain in 2001 by Chrysalis Children's Books
An imprint of Chrysalis Books Group Plc
The Chrysalis Building,
Bramley Road,
London W10 6SP

Paperback edition first published in 2003
Copyright © David Jefferis 2001

Design and editorial production Alpha Communications
Educational advisor Julie Stapleton
Picture research Kay Rowley

All rights reserved. No part of this book may be reproduced or utilized in any form or by any means, electronic or mechanical, including photocopying, recording or by any information storage and retrieval system, without permission in writing from the publisher, except by a reviewer who may quote brief passages in a review.

ISBN 1 84138 347 3 (hb)
ISBN 1 84138 764 9 (pb)

British Library Cataloguing in Publication Data for this book is available from the British Library.

Printed in China
10 9 8 7 6 5 4 3 2 1 (hb)
10 9 8 7 6 5 4 3 2   (pb)

Acknowledgements
We wish to thank the following individuals and organizations for their help and assistance and for supplying material in their collections:
Action-Plus Photographic, All Sport, All Sport USA, Alpha Archive, Steve Bardens, Mark Buscail, John Cleare, J. Corripio, Chris Craggs, David Davies, Bernard Giani, John Gichigi, M. Glaister, Nick Groves, Harry How, Tadashi Kajiyama, David Keaton, Duncan McCallum, Mountain Camera
Picture Library, PGL Boreatton Park, Mike Powell, Ian Smith, J. Stock, Stockshot, Pascal Tournaire, Vandystadt Photo Agency, E. Williams

Diagrams by Gavin Page

Take care of yourself!
Mountains can be dangerous places.
NEVER go for a walk without telling an adult where you are going.
NEVER go climbing without an expert to tell you what to do.

Contents

 Look out for the Super Sports symbol
Look for the equipment silhouette in boxes like this.
Here you will find extra mountain sport facts, stories
and useful tips for beginners.

World of mountain sports

▲ After a hard climb to reach the top, this climber is able to take some time to look at the fantastic view!

Mountain sports are exciting. They require good equipment and lots of teamwork.

Mountain sports are not just about climbing up to the very top of a mountain. Many people like to walk, hike or scramble up lower slopes for the fresh air and exercise.

Mountainous areas can be dangerous, so safety and survival skills are important on all trips.

▶ An expert and two beginners get ready for some climbing.

▲ Basic climbing skills are often taught at adventure camps.

◄ Climbers tackle steep cliffs and rocky slopes. They also cope with icy cold and bad weather.

▶ Many people enjoy the challenge of rock climbing.

Walk or scramble?

Many people are keen to stay on marked paths when they go hill walking. Others like to leave the track and scramble among the rocks.

▲ Anyone out on a hill or mountain has to plan for bad weather by taking suitable clothes and equipment.

A walk in the mountains needs planning. A travel kit like the one below is a good idea. It is sensible to leave a note of the route and expected time of return.

Scrambling is more effort than walking, but not as hard as climbing. Scramblers use their hands to help pull themselves up slopes. A rope may be used for safety on difficult parts. It is much like mountaineering was in the early nineteenth century, when climbers had only simple equipment. They made do with warm clothes, tough boots, ropes and a walking stick.

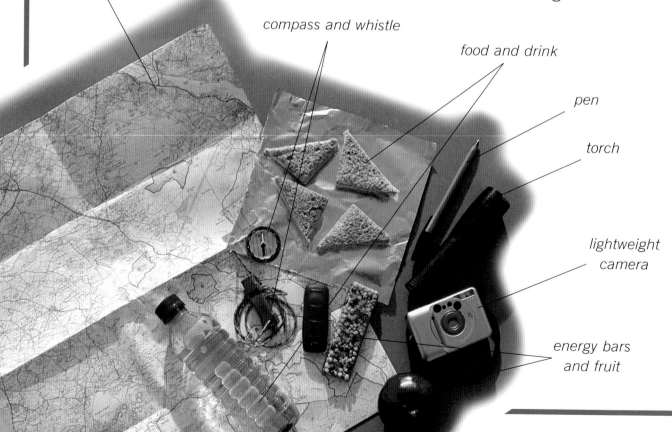

up-to-date map

compass and whistle

food and drink

pen

torch

lightweight camera

energy bars and fruit

▲ Protection from hot sun is very important. Walkers often wear a hat and protect their skin with sun-block cream.

◄ Even a short trip could include this equipment. Use the pen to mark a route on the map, which you should be able to read well. Instead of the hand torch, you could try a head type. It is strapped around the forehead, keeping both hands free. Use a small camera to record highlights.

Caring for the environment

Hills and mountains are beautiful places. Keep them that way by remembering some easy tips:

√ Do close gates after you go through them, even if they were open when you went in.

√ Do keep clear of wild animals. Most stay away, but some are dangerous if cornered.

√ Do put litter, tins and bottles in a bag. An animal or another climber may get cut by the sharp edges.

√ Do bury food waste in the ground if it will rot. If in doubt, bag it up with other litter and take it home.

√ Don't pick wild flowers or plants.

√ Don't write or carve your name on rocks or trees, or leave graffiti anywhere.

Mountain trails

Exploring high mountain trails is a good adventure sport for people who like to get away from crowded towns and cities.

▲ Water melted from mountain ice often forms blue-green lakes. This one is in the Canadian Rocky Mountains.

Many walkers and scramblers like to walk in remote places, far away from busy roads and towns.

Some countries make such treks easy. For example, in Switzerland there is a system of well-kept hiking paths. These take walkers over hundreds of mountain passes and through grassy valleys.

► Trekkers in Nepal look at some of the world's highest mountains.

◄ Early-morning sun lights mountain tops long before it reaches down into valleys.

Look out for mountain creatures

Many animals live in mountain country, but they usually keep away from humans.

Birds are quite easy to spot. They include eagles and buzzards, which circle in the sky while looking down for food. You may also see mountain goats on tracks that are too steep and narrow for people.

goats trot along mountain paths

birds use air currents to stay in flight

Mountain camp

The best camping gear is strong and light in weight. It should also be easy to use in awkward spots or in bad weather.

Picking a good camp site is important, even if it's only for one night. Experienced campers try to avoid places that will get boggy if it rains.

In high places, the main aim for a camper is to try and find a sheltered spot, with some protection from icy gales or heavy rain.

A modern lightweight tent is usually easy to put up, but it's always a good idea to practise at home first, to see how it works.

▲ In some countries, campers in forests hang food between trees, away from tents. Hungry animals are then less likely to come near the camp site.

Remember to take a first-aid kit

Bad injuries are rare, but cuts and grazes are common. It's always a good idea to carry a simple first-aid kit.

Items to take include sticking plasters and cream for blisters or cuts and grazes. Lint and surgical tape are useful for bigger wounds. A pair of tweezers is good for removing splinters and thorns.

items stay clean in a small zip bag

◀ A camper cooks a meal using a small gas stove. The stove uses fuel from a screw-in cylinder. The campers sit on a plastic-foam sleeping mat so they do not get wet.

▼ A nylon tent gives shelter at night. This is a lightweight model that can be packed away easily for carrying.

tent folds away into a small bag

Weather watch

Being prepared is the best way to stay safe in the mountains. Skilled climbers always check for changes in the weather.

▲ Bad weather may close in very quickly, so being aware of changes in the weather is important.

People who love the mountains usually become very good at reading the sky for signs of changing weather. It's not unusual for a storm to brew up in less than an hour, so trekkers and climbers always need weatherproof clothes.

A whistle can be used to signal for help – the distress sign is six long blasts, repeated after a minute. At night, even a small torch may be a life-saver if there are cliffs or steep drops nearby. To avoid getting lost, up-to-date maps and a compass should always be carried.

▲ Climbers lose a lot of water when they sweat, so they need plenty of drinks to replace it.

a good supply of water is essential, especially in hot weather

Moving air cools your skin faster than still air, which is why a breeze on a hot day feels so good.

In cold weather, a wind makes us feel even colder, an effect called wind-chill. In icy weather, frostbite is a danger.

The best way to fight wind-chill is to wear windproof and waterproof clothing, with gloves to keep fingers warm.

◀ Special gloves and clothing keep this climber warm in snow and ice.

Abseiling

Abseiling is a quick way to go down a steep cliff or rock face, using ropes to control the speed of the descent.

Many adventure sports camps teach abseiling. These are good places to learn, as expert instructors are on hand to make sure that nothing goes wrong.

Abseiling is a way to get past a difficult overhang that has few hand or foot holds. It is also a fast way to go down a rock face if the weather starts to change for the worse. But in all conditions, especially in bad weather, abseiling has to be done with great care.

◄ Here a beginner learns to abseil down a rock face. The ropes are clipped to a harness, worn round the waist and thighs.

instructor makes sure the descent is carried out safely

▲ It is important to wear safety helmets, even on easy practice rocks.

The first time is tough!

Abseiling off the edge of a rock face is a test of nerves.

You stand on top of a rock face and lean backwards, trusting that the ropes won't break.

Then you slowly edge out until your feet go over the edge. Then it is easy to walk down the slope.

Starting off

Climbing is more about technique and skill than strength and muscle power. Beginners can learn some basic skills in just a few days.

Climbers start off by standing back to see where the climb goes. They also look for rock features that will make good hand and foot holds on the way up.

Beginners soon learn to tie knots, and to use ropes and clip them on to a nylon harness. A harness makes climbing easier and safer.

▲ It's the first time up a rock face for this beginner. The instructor (top) holds the safety rope, and points out the best hand and foot holds.

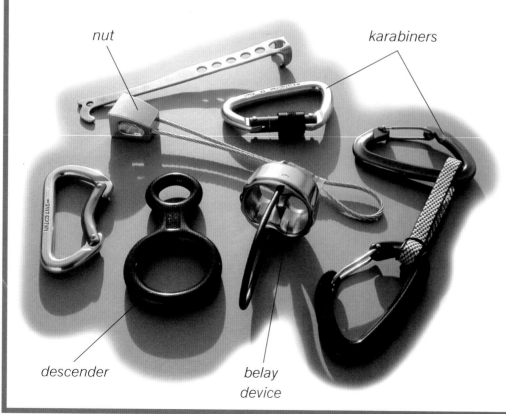

nut

karabiners

descender

belay device

◀ Here are some tools used by rock climbers. A nut can be wedged in a crack to hold a rope. A karabiner is a metal clip that links a climber to a rope. Descenders and belay devices are used when abseiling.

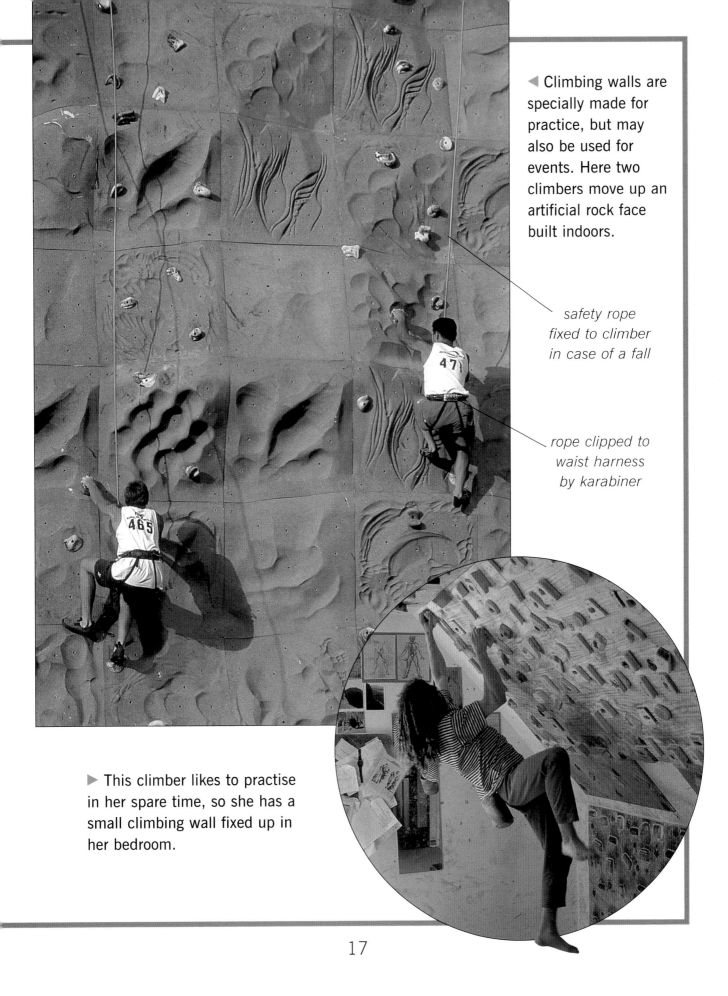

◀ Climbing walls are specially made for practice, but may also be used for events. Here two climbers move up an artificial rock face built indoors.

safety rope fixed to climber in case of a fall

rope clipped to waist harness by karabiner

▶ This climber likes to practise in her spare time, so she has a small climbing wall fixed up in her bedroom.

Bouldering

Bouldering is the sport of climbing large rocks without using any equipment. It is a good way for climbers to practise their skills.

▲ This outcrop of rock is just right for climbing practice.

The great thing about bouldering is that a climber needs no safety equipment, because the idea is to go no higher than it is safe to jump off.

Many climbers use boulders for fun and for practice. They can climb up using various routes, and work out climbing methods, such as a way to get up a rock face in a certain time.

▶ This boulder was pushed into the valley by a glacier thousands of years ago. Today an expert climber practises on it. The top of the rock is too high for children though!

Beware loose rocks!

Climbers soon learn that most rock faces have some loose or unsafe parts. There are easy ways to check if a hand hold is safe, including wobbling a hold to see if it will take your weight.

One climber in the Italian Alps who did not check a hold had a nasty surprise. A big chunk of cliff face broke free, and all he could do as he slid down was to push into the loose rock with his hands and feet. Luckily there was enough grip, and he was safe.

chalk soaks up sweat from hot hands

◀ Rock climbers may sprinkle chalk on their hands for grip.

Ice and snow

An ice axe and spiked crampons are essential pieces of equipment for climbers who enjoy tackling snow-covered mountain peaks.

◀ A climber climbs a frozen wall, using ice axe and crampons to move upwards.

The top of an ice axe is called the head. It has a sharp pick at one end and a flat spade, called an adze, at the other. The adze is useful for digging or cutting holds, while the pick can be used as a hook.

A crampon is a spiked frame fixed to a boot. Sharp spikes on the bottom and front give a firm grip on ice.

spikes in the crampons dig into the ice

Different kinds of snow

Snow is one of the most changeable things in nature. It ranges from a soft, dry powder to firm snow that may be almost as hard as ice.

Climbing through deep, soft snow is slow work, even for a team. The leader does most of the hard work, making either steps or a trough for the other climbers to use.

Experienced teams change the lead often, so no single climber does all the hard work.

▲ An avalanche is a mass of loose snow and ice that roars down a mountain side. Any climber who is in the way may be swept away or buried.

◄ A frozen waterfall looks like a difficult climb. In fact, on this one there are lots of hand and foot holds, and plenty of grip for the two ice axes.

Roof of the world

Most of the world's highest mountains are in the Himalayas. This huge range is in Asia, between India and China.

▲ Himalayan expeditions often make several camps on their way up to the summit of a mountain.

Climbing really high mountains is very different from day-to-day climbing. Above 2500m, most people become breathless and tired. The air is so thin that climbers may spend a week just getting used to it, before they can start to climb.

Bad weather may prevent a start for days, even weeks, as no expedition wants to be trapped on a mountain in a blizzard.

◄ Climbers are roped securely when abseiling among high peaks.

Highest mountain in the world

Mount Everest is the highest mountain in the Himalayas. Climbers first reached its 8848m summit in 1953.

At this height the air is very thin, and almost all climbers who have tackled Everest have used a special air supply for breathing. The equipment is made up of a face mask, joined by rubber hose to a backpack air tank.

▲ Climbers make their way slowly towards the summit of Mt Everest.

New ideas

Designers are always improving climbing equipment. Better materials lead to lighter, yet stronger gear. Satellite systems help with navigation.

▲ Cheap air travel makes it easier for people to go trekking in faraway places.

New equipment makes mountain sports easier. For example, the latest karabiners weigh far less than older steel types, yet are much stronger.

Modern clothing is better, too. Fabrics now keep a climber warm, yet allow body moisture to escape.

New mountain sports appear from time to time. Solo climbing is one of these. Here a climber tackles an ascent alone, without using high-tech equipment.

▼ A solo climber crosses a rock face.

 High-tech navigation

The GPS (global positioning system) computerized navigator can make life simpler for people in the mountains. GPS uses a system of satellites to work out an exact position, anywhere on Earth. This model is the size of a mobile phone, and shows position, height and direction. Even so, it is no replacement for old-fashioned skills with a map and compass!

GPS screen shows height and position

◄ One thing stays the same – the thrill of getting to the top!

Mountain sport facts

▲ The first climbers to reach the summit of Mt Everest were Edmund Hillary (left) and Tenzing Norgay.

Here are some facts and stories from the world of mountain sports

Highest mountain

The world's highest mountain is Mount Everest in the Himalayas. It lies on the borders of Tibet and Nepal. Everest is 8848m high, and was first climbed in 1953.

No oxygen

The first climbers up Everest carried air bottles, because of the thin air. But in 1978 Reinhold Messner and Peter Habeler managed to climb the mountain without any air supplies at all.

◀ Mt Blanc is the tallest mountain in the Alps, at 4807m high. It was first climbed in 1786.

Haunted heights

In the Middle Ages, many people thought mountains were haunted by ghosts. In Germany people claimed to see ghostly figures near the Brocken, a peak in the Harz Mountains. In fact, the 'ghosts' were shadows on misty clouds, cast by the sun at certain times of day!

First climbers

There was very little sport mountaineering before 1850. But between 1854 and 1865, many Alpine peaks were climbed for the first time. By 1900 climbers had tackled many of the highest mountains around the world.

◄ Climbers make their way across a tangle of fallen ice. They are roped together for safety.

So you like heights?

Above 2500m there are all sorts of health risks. Feeling dizzy and sick is common, caused by lack of oxygen in the air. A sore, bleeding nose may be caused by the dry air.

Wrecking the rocks

In the 1960s, many climbers used hard-steel pegs to fix their lines. Many rock faces were chipped away by these pegs. People today mostly climb 'clean', using tools that are kinder to the environment.

Heavy to light...

A century ago, climbers wore thick clothes and heavy, nailed boots. A big wooden axe, called an alpenstock, was carried. As climbing became more popular, so equipment was improved. The alpenstock developed into the modern lightweight ice axe. Early crampons were first used in the 1800s.

Five days up a cliff

The world's highest sea-cliff is the Thumbnail, in Greenland. It comes out of the sea, rising for 1368m. Four climbers tackled the cliff in 2000. It took them five days to reach the top, and they had to rent a dinghy in order to get to the start of the climb!

Fastest down Everest

Davo Karnicar took a month to climb Everest in 2000, but he came down in less than five hours. How? He was the first person to ski down!

...and lighter still

The tiny Pocket Rocket camping stove is a trekker's delight. It weighs just 86g, which is less than a small apple. When plugged in to a gas cylinder, it can boil a litre of water in a few minutes.

◄ Mt Everest is the highest mountain in the world. Lower down its slopes are many glaciers.

Mountain sport words

▲ A karabiner holds a rope.

Here are some technical terms used in this book.

abseil

A method of coming down a rock face or overhang, using a rope and usually a harness.

alpenstock

A type of wooden axe used by early climbers.

anchor

Point of attachment. It can be a natural anchor, such as a rock, or a tool, such as a nut.

avalanche

A mass of snow or ice that breaks loose from a mountain, rushing down at high speed.

belay

To make the rope secure so that a fall is prevented.

blizzard

A violent storm with driving snow and wind.

bouldering

Climbing a large rock (or small cliff) without having to use a rope or other safety equipment. The idea is to go no higher up the boulder than it is safe to jump off.

climbing wall

Artificial wall, with moulded hand and foot holds. Most walls are built indoors and are used for year-round training.

crampon

A metal frame that can be attached to a climbing boot. Crampons have spikes that point down and forward. They are used to give grip on ice and hard snow.

face

Any large area of rock, snow or ice that is unbroken or that has few features sticking out.

frostbite

Damage to the body caused by icy chill. In extreme cold, blood may stop flowing to body parts such as fingers, toes and ears. When this happens, the tissue dies and the affected area may have to be removed.

◀ A climber looks for hand holds on a rock face.

◄ The Athabaska glacier flows in the Canadian Rocky Mountains. The bottom end of such a glacier is called the snout.

— snout

glacier
A huge mass of ice that flows slowly down a mountain. The melting lower parts feed streams and rivers.

GPS
Short for Global Positioning System, a number of satellites that send radio signals down to the Earth. A GPS receiver picks up these signals and can record its position anywhere on our planet.

harness
A piece of equipment that joins a climber to a rope, and spreads the load in a fall. It may be a sit-harness, which is worn around the waist and thighs, or a full-body harness.

hold
Any part of rock or ice (such as a crack or outcrop) that can be used by the hands or feet for climbing.

ice axe
A tool used on snow and ice. It can be used for cutting, for digging, as an anchor, even for breaking a slide after a fall.

karabiner
An oval or D-shaped metal link with a spring or screw gate. Its main use is to join anchors to ropes.

◄ An ice axe is used on snow and ice.

lint
A piece of soft linen used to dress a wound.

nut
A metal tool which is wedged into a crack to hold a rope.

overhang
Any part of a rock or cliff face that sticks out beyond the rest of the surface.

oxygen
One of the gases in the air, which is essential for all animals, including humans.

solo climber
Someone who climbs alone and does not use ropes. Free climbers use a rope for safety but use natural holds.

sun-block cream
Cream rubbed on to exposed skin to reduce sunburn.

wind-chill
The effect of wind taking away heat from the body, so the skin feels colder than the surrounding air.

Mountain science

There is lots to learn about the world of mountains.

Cracking rocks

Mountains are slowly worn away over time by water, ice, wind and chemicals. When water seeps into a crack in a rock and freezes, the ice expands, or gets bigger. This forces the two sides of the rock apart, so that pieces break off.

◀ These rocks split into jagged pieces as ice gets to work inside cracks just below the surface.

Ice expands

This experiment shows you an unusual fact about water. Unlike most materials, which shrink as they get colder, water expands when it turns to ice.

1 You need an empty yoghurt pot, some water, a waterproof-ink marker pen and a fridge-freezer.

2 Mark a waterline clearly with the pen. Make this about 5 mm from the top of the pot.

Building mountains

Many mountains are formed when two parts of the Earth's surface push against each other. You can see the effect in this experiment. All you need are two sheets of plain paper.

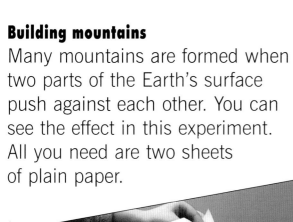

Asia
Himalayas

◀ India is slowly pushing against Asia. The Himalayas rise where the two land masses meet.

India

1 Fold the sheets carefully, to make them into zig-zag mountain shapes. Lay them out on a flat surface, next to each other.

2 Push the sheets slowly towards each other. As you push, the touching edges of the sheets should rise up, like mountains.

waterline mark below top of ice

125g℮

3 Carefully fill the yoghurt pot with water, up to the marked waterline.

4 Place the pot in the ice-making compartment of a refrigerater. Leave overnight.

5 Next morning, you will see that the top of the ice is above the line you marked.

Index